Superstars
of the
SAN FRANCISCO
GIANTS

by Annabelle Tometich

amicus
high interest

Amicus High Interest is published by Amicus
P.O. Box 1329, Mankato, MN 56002
www.amicuspublishing.us

Library of Congress Cataloging-in-Publication Data
Tometich, Annabelle, 1980-
  Superstars of the San Francisco Giants / by Annabelle Tometich.
    pages cm. -- (Pro sports superstars)
  Includes index.
  Summary: "Presents some of the San Francisco Giants' greatest players
and their achievements in pro baseball, including Tim Lincecum and
Buster Posey"--Provided by publisher.
  ISBN 978-1-60753-596-6 (hardcover) -- ISBN 978-1-60753-631-4 (pdf
ebook)
  1. San Francisco Giants (Baseball team)--History--Juvenile literature. I.
Title.
  GV875.S34T66 2014
  796.357'640979461--dc23
                        2013044096

Produced for Amicus by The Peterson Publishing Company
and Red Line Editorial.

Editor Arnold Ringstad
Designer Maggie Villaume
Printed in the United States of America
Mankato, MN
2-2014
PA10001
10 9 8 7 6 5 4 3 2 1

TABLE OF CONTENTS

MEET THE SAN FRANCISCO GIANTS

The Giants started in New York in 1883. The team moved to San Francisco in 1958. They have won two **World Series** there. The San Francisco Giants have had many stars. Here are some of the best.

6

WILLIE MAYS

Willie Mays is a baseball legend. He was a great outfielder. Mays played 21 seasons with the Giants. The first was in 1951. Mays played in 24 **All-Star Games**.

Mays could hit, run, throw, and catch. He is one of the best players ever.

ORLANDO CEPEDA

Orlando Cepeda played first base. He was a great hitter. He hit 226 **home runs** for the Giants. He was **Rookie of the Year** in 1958.

9

WILLIE MCCOVEY

Willie McCovey was a great hitter. He had a powerful swing. McCovey hit 18 **grand slams**. In 1969 he earned an **MVP** award.

A bay is behind the team's stadium. Fans call it McCovey Cove.

JUAN MARICHAL

Juan Marichal was a great pitcher. He kicked his leg high in the air for power. In 1963 Marichal pitched an amazing game. He pitched 16 innings. No batters got a hit.

WILL CLARK

Will Clark's nickname was "Will the Thrill." He had a smooth swing. Clark played in six All-Star Games. He played in the 1989 World Series.

MATT CAIN

Matt Cain is a skilled pitcher. In 2012 he pitched a perfect game. This means no one on the other team reached first base. Cain struck out 14 batters.

Perfect games are very rare. Cain's game was only the twenty-second in history.

TIM LINCECUM

Tim Lincecum is a strong pitcher.
Lincecum helped the Giants
win two World Series. The last
was in 2012. He has two **Cy
Young Awards**.

BUSTER POSEY

Buster Posey is a great catcher. He is also a strong hitter. In 2012, he drove in 103 runs. Posey helped the Giants win two World Series.

The Giants have had many great superstars. Who will be next?

Posey once played all nine positions in one college game.

TEAM FAST FACTS

Founded: 1883

Other names: New York Gothams (1883-1884), New York Giants (1885-1957)

Nicknames: The Orange and Black, Los Gigantes, The G-Men, The Boys from the Bay

Home Stadium: AT&T Park (San Francisco, California)

World Series Championships: 7 (1905, 1921, 1922, 1933, 1954, 2010, 2012)

Hall of Fame Players: 29, including Orlando Cepeda, Willie Mays, Willie McCovey, and Juan Marichal

WORDS TO KNOW

All-Star Games – games between the best players in baseball each year

Cy Young Awards – awards given to the best pitchers each year

grand slams – home runs hit when all three bases have runners on them, scoring four runs

home runs – hits that go far enough to leave the field, letting the hitter run all the way around the bases to score a run

MVP – Most Valuable Player; an honor given to the best player each season

Rookie of the Year – An award given to the best baseball players in their first year

World Series – the annual baseball championship series

LEARN MORE

Books

Gitlin, Marty. *San Francisco Giants (Inside MLB)*. Minneapolis, MN: Abdo Publishing, 2011.

Monnig, Alex. *San Francisco Giants (Favorite Baseball Teams)*. North Mankato, MN: Child's World, 2014.

Web Sites

Baseball History
http://mlb.mlb.com/mlb/history
Learn more about the history of baseball.

MLB.com
http://mlb.com
See pictures and track your favorite baseball player's stats.

San Francisco Giants—Official Site
http://sanfrancisco.giants.mlb.com
Watch video clips and read stories about the San Francisco Giants.

INDEX